G.I.F.T.S.

Empower Your Journey with Five Keys of Transformation

WORKBOOK

Elaine Lombardi

MEL BOOKS

MEL BOOKS
2234 Via Puerta, Unit H
Laguna Woods, CA 92637

Copyright © 2024 by Elaine Lombardi

All rights reserved. No part of this publication may be reproduced, distributed, or transmitted in any form or by any means, including photocopying, recording, or other electronic or mechanical methods without the prior written permission of the publisher, except in the case of brief quotation embodied in critical reviews and certain other noncommercial use permitted by copyright law. For permission requests contact the Author Elaine Lombardi.

Email: elaine@elainelombardi.com
Website: www.ElaineLombardi.com
ISBN : 978-0-9861287-9-0
FIRST EDITION, 2024

Library of Congress Cataloging-in-Publication Data
Lombardi, Elaine
G.I.F.T.S. Empower Your Journey with Five Keys of Transformation Workbook

Summary: Insightful strategies for embarking on a journey to heal childhood wounds and unlock a newfound sense of purpose, passion, joy, and fulfillment by using the five golden keys that led to the formation of the G.I.F.T.S. method stratagies in this workbook.

Cover Design by: Amina N.
Interior Design by: Saleh Joy

The content of this workbook is for general instructions only. Each person's physical, emotional, and spiritual condition is unique. The instructions in this workbook are not intended to replace or interrupt the reader's relationship with a physician or other professional. Please consult your doctor for matters about your specific health and wellness.

Lombardi, Elaine

G.I.F.T.S. Empower Your Journey with the Five Keys of Transformation Workbook / Elaine Lombardi – First Edition

ISBN: 978-0-9861287-9-0 (trade pbk: alk paper) 1. Purpose 2. Passion 3. Fulfillment 4 Transformation 5. Childhood Trauma 6. Well-Being I. Lombardi, Elaine   II. Title

Printed in the United States of America

THIS WORKBOOK BELONGS TO

_____

Contents

INTRODUCTION	1
ROOTS OF INFLUENCE	
1 My Childhood Memories	3
2 Stages of My Childhood	6
3 My Motivations, Values, and Beliefs	7
4 Using Visualization with Affirmations	11
5 Journaling Guidelines	12
THE G.I.F.T.S. METHOD	
6 Five Keys of Transformation	15
KEY OF GRATITUDE	
7 Gratitude	17
8 Cultivating My Gratitude Practice	19
KEY OF INTUITIVE INTENTION	
9 Being the Architect of My Life	21
10 My Ego vs My Soul	24
11 Self-Sabotaging Behaviors	25
KEY OF FAMILY AND FRIENDS	
12 My Relationship with Family and Friends	26
13 My Personality Development	29
14 Self-Worth, Self-Confidence, and Self-Esteem	31
15 Strengthening My Communication	33
16 Strategies for a Healthy, Long-Lasting Relationship	34

KEY OF TREASURED WISDOM

    17 Embracing My Passions   38

    18 Journey to Unlock My Treasured Wisdom   40

    19 My Best Day Ever   42

KEY OF SELF-LOVE & CARE

    20 Self-Love & Care   44

    21 Rejuvenating Sleep Ritual   45

    22 Mindful Healthy Eating Habits   46

    23 Exercise Made Easy   48

    24 Personal Care   49

    25 Designing A Nurturing Self Care Plan   50

    26 My Path to Purpose Passion, Joy, and Fulfillment   52

CONCLUSION   54

About The Author   *55*

INTRODUCTION

Welcome to the G.I.F.T.S. method workbook. Your companion guide on the Journey of Transformation. Congratulations on taking the first step toward unlocking the profound gifts within you. This workbook is designed to be your companion as you delve deeper into the concepts and exercises outlined in the print book, *GIFTS: Empower Your Journey with Five Keys of Transformation*. This journey is not just about finding answers but about asking yourself the right questions and embracing the power of self-discovery.

In the print book, we explore how your childhood experiences shape the way you navigate the world as an adult. We acknowledge the wounds you may carry and find the courage to heal them. This workbook provides you with a dedicated space to journal your thoughts, reflect on your experiences, and engage with the questions posed in the book.

What to Expect

Throughout this workbook, you will revisit the five golden keys that make up the G.I.F.T.S. method:

1. **Gratitude**: Cultivate a positive mindset by appreciating the blessings in your life and releasing limiting beliefs.

2. **Intuitive Intention**: Align your actions with your inner wisdom and values, making mindful choices that honor your well-being and authenticity.

3. **Family and Friends**: Foster meaningful connections and support networks that are essential for emotional and spiritual growth.

4. **Treasured Wisdom**: Seek knowledge and insights that nourish your soul, and share your generational wisdom with others.

5. **Self-Love & Care**: Prioritize self-care and self-compassion, cultivating a deep sense of worthiness and inner peace.

Elaine Lombardi

How to Use This Workbook

This workbook is structured to follow the same questions and topics as the print book. Each section provides prompts and space for journaling, encouraging you to reflect deeply on your journey. As you work through the exercises, take your time to explore your thoughts and emotions fully. There are no right or wrong answers—only your authentic experiences and insights.

A Journey of Healing and Growth

As you embark on this journey, remember that healing and growth are processes. Be gentle with yourself and embrace the changes that come. This workbook is here to support you every step of the way, offering a safe space to express yourself and uncover the profound impact of your transformation.

Imagine a future where you stand tall in the face of adversity, guided by intentions fueled by your innate intuition and unwavering determination. Picture yourself surrounded by heart-centered relationships that uplift and inspire you, propelling you forward on your journey with courage and grace.

Your Story Matters

Your journey is unique, and this workbook is a testament to the resilience of the human spirit and the infinite potential for growth within each of us. The insights and wisdom you gather here will not only transform your life but also contribute positively to the world around you.

As you begin this transformative journey, know that you are not alone. You are part of a community of individuals committed to living purposeful, joyful, and fulfilling lives. Together, we can unlock our inner wisdom and embrace the power of the GIFTS method. Let's begin your journey of self-discovery and transformation by first getting clear about what you remember about your childhood. The following exercises are taken directly from the G.I.F.T.S. book.

1
My Childhood Memories

There is no such thing as a perfect childhood. Your upbringing is unique, and your childhood is shaped by a variety of factors including; your family dynamics, interactions at school, relationships with peers, exposure to media, societal norms, socioeconomic status, cultural background, and your own temperament.

Self Reflection Questions

As you reflect on your childhood memories, I invite you to pause and consider the following questions:

What are some of the earliest recollections that stand out most vividly in your mind?

_____
_____
_____
_____
_____
_____
_____

Can you recall specific sensations, sights, or sounds that take you back to those formative years?

_____
_____
_____
_____
_____
_____
_____

Elaine Lombardi

How do these memories, whether joyful or challenging, continue to influence your perspectives and behaviors today?

_____
_____
_____
_____
_____
_____
_____

Journaling Exercise

Take a moment to journal about one or two of your most impactful childhood experiences. Describe the setting, the emotions you felt, and how that moment has shaped the person you are today. By connecting with your personal history in this way, you can begin to uncover the impact of your early life experiences. Taking the time to examine your childhood memories, both positive and negative, empowers you to gain a deeper understanding of the root beliefs, that drive your behaviors, and contribute to your sense of self.

_____
_____
_____
_____
_____
_____
_____
_____
_____
_____

The Negativity Bias

The human brain has a natural tendency to pay more attention to negative stimuli than positive ones. This bias, often referred to as the negativity bias, evolved as a survival mechanism to help us detect and respond to potential threats in our environment. As a result, negative experiences may leave a more significant imprint on our memory and cognition, leading us to recall them more readily than positive experiences.

Dwelling on negative experiences from childhood may serve as a coping mechanism for unresolved emotional issues or trauma. Revisiting these memories may also offer a sense of validation or control over past events.

Revisiting Happy Memories

Positive memories from your childhood can serve as reminders of your capacity to overcome challenges and find joy in life's simple pleasures. By recalling moments of resilience, accomplishment, and happiness, you will reinforce your belief in your ability to navigate adversity and thrive in the face of adversity.

Write a happy memory story

_____

_____

_____

_____

_____

_____

_____

_____

_____

_____

_____

_____

_____

_____

2
Stages of My Childhood

From infancy, where biological and early caregiver interactions lay the foundation, to adolescence, where biological changes, social dynamics, and identity exploration become paramount. Each stage plays a crucial role in shaping your identity, beliefs, and behaviors.

Self Reflection Questions

As you reflect on the different stages of your childhood jot down what stands out about each stage.

Infant and Toddler Years?

_____
_____
_____
_____

Elementary School Years?

_____
_____
_____
_____
_____

High School and Teenage Years?

_____
_____
_____
_____
_____

3
My Motivations, Values & Beliefs

As you navigate life's ups and downs, your values and beliefs may naturally shift. As a starting point start with where you are at right now. Consider the activities, experiences, or causes that ignite a fire within you, and make you feel the most alive and engaged.

Self Reflection Questions

Tune into your inner compass by asking yourself the following questions.

What brings me a deep sense of purpose and fulfillment?

_____

_____

Am I motivated by a desire to help others? Create something meaningful? Live a life of adventure and exploration?

_____

_____

_____

Examining your thoughts, emotions, and behaviors with clarity and objectivity involves recognizing your strengths and weaknesses.

What emotions arise as I revisit moments from my past?

_____

_____

_____

Are there patterns or themes I notice about my thoughts and behaviors?

_____

_____

_____

Shining a light on patterns you notice can reveal their origins and how they continue to influence your life today.

Was I taught to value communication and emotional intimacy, or was I surrounded by examples of dysfunction and conflict?

_____

_____

Was I encouraged to pursue my passions and dreams, or was I made to feel inadequate or unworthy of love and acceptance?

_____

_____

Decoding Values and Beliefs

Values represent what you hold dear and aspire to / whereas **beliefs** represent your understanding and interpretation of reality.

Values guide your choices and actions / whereas **beliefs** inform your perspectives.

Steps to Overcoming Limiting Beliefs

STEP ONE: Identify Your Beliefs

The first step in overcoming limiting beliefs is to identify them.

What do I believe? _____

_____

STEP TWO: Challenge Your Beliefs

Once identified, challenge your belief logically and rationally. Ask yourself:

Challenge fact vs. fiction

1. Is this belief based on fact or is it based on fear?
2. What specific experiences or observations led to this belief?
3. Is there concrete evidence to support this belief?
4. Are there instances where this belief has been disproven or challenged?

Challenge the driving force

5. What emotions (fear of failure, rejection, inadequacy) are associated with this belief?

6. How does this belief protect or validate these fears or insecurities

Challenge the outcome

7. Observe yourself and others objectively and assess the outcome.

8. Identify instances where you have succeeded or performed well.

9. Look for examples of others who have achieved success in a similar situation.

Is this belief true or false? and Why? _____

_____

STEP THREE: Replace Your Limiting Beliefs

Repeatedly saying thoughtful positive affirmations is a powerful technique used to replace false and limiting beliefs by reinforcing positive new beliefs.

1. I release all limiting beliefs from my childhood and embrace my true potential.
2. I am worthy of love, success, and happiness, regardless of my past experiences.
3. I let go of any belief that I am not enough, and I fully accept myself as I am.
4. I am capable of achieving my dreams and creating the life I desire.
5. I choose to see challenges as opportunities for growth and learning.
6. I release the need to seek approval from others and trust in my own worth.
7. I am deserving of abundance in all areas of my life.
8. I believe in my abilities and have the confidence to pursue my passions.
9. I release any fear of failure and embrace the journey of self-discovery.
10. I am free to create new, empowering beliefs that align with my highest potential.

Use this space to check in with yourself. What progress am I making? What challenges do I still have and need to work on improving?

_____

_____

_____

Limiting Beliefs Worksheet

copy and print

What do I believe? _____

Is this belief true or false? and Why? _____

_____

_____

Affirmation to replace limiting belief? _____

_____

What do I believe? _____

Is this belief true or false? and Why? _____

_____

_____

Affirmation to replace this limiting belief? _____

What do I believe?_____

Is this belief true or false? and Why?_____

_____

_____

Affirmation to replace this limiting belief? _____

What do I believe?_____ _____

_____

Is this belief true or false? and Why? _____

_____

_____

Affirmation to replace this limiting belief? _____

4
Using Visualization with Affirmations

Affirmations combined with visualization create a dynamic synergy that amplifies personal growth and manifestation. While affirmations empower your beliefs and attitudes, when paired with vivid mental imagery through visualization your affirmations become more potent.

STEP ONE: Mindful Selection of Affirmations

Choosing affirmations that align with your personal goals and values is the first crucial step.

Example

1. I am worthy of love and kindness.
2. I radiate confidence, self-respect, and inner harmony.
3. I am in control of my thoughts, and I choose positivity

STEP TWO: Repetition and Visualization

Consistent daily practice reinforces the positive messages, gradually replacing old thought patterns with your new desired affirmative thoughts. Visualization further enhances the effectiveness of your affirmations by engaging your brain in creating vivid mental images associated with the positive statements you say. *Example*

Affirmation: "I am worthy of love and kindness."

Visualization: Imagine yourself surrounded by a warm, golden light, symbolizing love and kindness. Feel this light enveloping you, starting from the top of your head and flowing down to your toes. Visualize yourself basking in this loving energy, feeling worthy, cherished, and deeply loved. See yourself embracing this feeling of worthiness and kindness, allowing it to fill every part of your being.

STEP THREE: Integration

Methods such as the following all serve as constant reminders.

1. Recite affirmations during meditation
2. Say them to yourself in the mirror during your morning routine
3. Do a visualization right before bedtime can be very effective.
4. Write down your affirmations and post them in a prominent location.

Write an affirmation to practice visualizing

_____

5
Journaling Guidelines

Journaling is a powerful practice that involves using writing as a tool for personal growth, self-reflection, and self-improvement. Through journaling, you can explore your thoughts, emotions, beliefs, and experiences in a structured and intentional way.

Choose Your Journal

Choosing the right journal is a personal decision that depends on your intended use.

1. Do you want a journal that includes dedicated space for daily entries and/or space to journal your thoughts freely without headlines?
2. Do you want prompts to guide you in writing your thoughts and feelings?
3. Do you prefer a lined or a blank-page journal you can also draw in?
4. Is a spiral-bound journal or notebook for easy flipping important to you?
5. What size and price will work best for you and your budget?

Getting Started

STEP ONE: **Set the Mood**

Find a comfortable and quiet space where you feel relaxed and inspired.

STEP TWO: **Clear Your Mind**

Practice deep breathing, meditation, or a short mindfulness exercise to quiet any distractions and prepare your mind for writing.

STEP THREE: **Choose Your Topic**

Decide what you want to write about. Choose a topic that interests you and sparks your curiosity.

STEP FOUR: **Set a Goal**

Set a specific goal or intention to help keep you focused and motivated.

STEP FIVE: **Start Writing**

Let your thoughts flow freely onto the page without judgment or editing. If you're feeling stuck, try using writing prompts or doodling until something comes to mind that you feel compelled to write about.

Let's explore some topics

- **Gratitude** journaling is a simple yet powerful practice of writing what you are thankful for.
- **Relationship** journaling focuses on writing about the connections you have with others.
- **Storytelling** journalling can be a make-believe fantasy or an expression of your deepest desires.

Use the space below to practice writing about a topic that interests you.

TOPIC:

_____
_____
_____
_____
_____
_____
_____
_____
_____

Use the space below to write freely without line or try your hand at doodling.

Which style of journaling do I prefer? _____

_____

6
Five Keys of Transformation

At the heart of the G.I.F.T.S. method are five golden keys, each representing an essential aspect of living a fulfilling and joyous life. The term **G.I.F.T.S.** serves as an acronym for **G**ratitude, intuitive **I**ntention, your relationships with **F**amily and friends, your **T**reasured wisdom, and **S**elf-love & Care. These five key aspects of life work together to unlock a realm of gifts and new possibilities for you, which guide you toward a deeper sense of wholeness and balanced harmony within yourself and the world around you.

The G.I.F.T.S. method is a unified system designed to empower you to uncover the habits and mindsets that will truly transform your life in a meaningful way. It goes beyond quick fixes and temporary solutions to create lasting change from the inside out. With the G.I.F.T.S. method, you'll learn how to cultivate positive habits and mindsets that lead to a more balanced, purpose-driven, and joyous existence. This roadmap guides you toward a life that feels fulfilling and authentic.

Whether you're looking to improve your relationships, find more meaning in your work, or simply live with more joy and vitality, the G.I.F.T.S. method can help. It's a comprehensive approach that addresses key aspects of your life, giving you the tools and support you need to thrive. I invite you to step into your power and create the life you've always dreamed of. I am here to support you every step of the way. It's time to unlock your full potential and live a life that truly brings you joy and fulfillment.

Imagine waking up each day to a life where you are truly seen, heard, respected, and acknowledged for the wonderful person you are. Picture yourself radiating with positive energy, sending out ripples of warmth and kindness that touch the lives of everyone you encounter. In this life, you possess the power to create a truly gratifying and purposeful existence. It's a life where love flows freely, where every experience is an opportunity for growth and learning, and where heartfelt connections with others enrich your journey. Just imagine the possibilities that lie before you when you embrace your true self and live authentically.

You can shape your reality and create a world where love and compassion reign supreme. Every smile you share, every kind word you speak, every act of generosity you extend. These are the building blocks of the life you've always dreamed of. And within you, deep in your heart and soul, lies the potential to turn that dream into a beautiful reality. So don't hold back. Let your light shine brightly for all to see.

As you unlock and embrace each of the five golden keys within the G.I.F.T.S. method, you'll begin to see positive changes unfold in your life. Within you lies the power to create a gratifying and purposeful well-lived life that leaves a legacy of heartfelt connections and admiration.

Embrace the love and joy that surrounds you, and let it guide you toward a life filled with purpose, fulfillment, and heartfelt connections. The world is waiting for you to step into your greatness, and the possibilities are endless.

Key of Gratitude

Unlock the gift of appreciating the blessings in your life by cultivating a positive mindset. Through the daily practice of focusing on the positives, you shift your perspective by embracing the healing potential of positive thinking, which in turn radiates positivity and gratitude to those around you.

Key of Intuitive Intention

Unlock the gift of mindful choices and being the architect of your life. Empower yourself to make mindful choices that honor your well-being and authenticity, allowing you to live a passion-rich, purpose-driven life.

Key of Family and Friends

Unlock the gift of meaningful connections with family and friends. Discovering the importance of connection and support in fostering emotional and spiritual growth become essential pillars in your healing journey. Through these relationships, you learn the power of empathy and compassion that extends beyond yourself.

Key of Treasured Wisdom

Unlock the gift of knowledge and insightful wisdom that nourish your soul and uncover the treasure trove of generational wisdom collected within yourself, which you are blessed to share with others and contribute to the collective wisdom of humanity.

Key of Self-love and Care

Unlock the gift of prioritizing yourself through self-care practices and embracing self-compassion. Through nurturing these practices, you cultivate a deep sense of worthiness and inner peace, which enables you to show up more fully for others and contribute positively to your community and the world.

7
Gratitude

Gratitude is a fundamental element that contributes to a sense of balance, well-being, and fulfillment. The key to unlocking the gifts of gratitude is appreciating the blessings in your life and cultivating a positive mindset. Through daily gratitude practice, you shift your perspective by embracing the healing potential of positive thinking, much like affirmations, which in turn radiates positivity, with gratitude extending to those around you.

During challenging times, feeling grateful isn't always easy or straightforward. The complexities of life can overshadow your ability to recognize the good around you.

What's one challenge that makes me doubt my ability to feel grateful?

_____

_____

_____

Know this: Gratitude doesn't require you to ignore pain or dismiss your struggles. During times of deep distress, it's important to allow yourself to experience all your emotions without guilt. Feeling overwhelmed doesn't diminish your appreciation for the positive aspects of your life or the love from those around you. Give yourself the grace and space to navigate through your emotions without self-judgment.

Discovering Silver Linings

Even in tough times, there's a silver lining hidden behind the clouds. Discovering silver linings means noticing unexpected positives from difficult situations such as growing stronger, feeling closer to loved ones, or learning important life lessons.

What positive aspects or silver linings can I find among my challenges?

_____

_____

_____

_____

Gratitude and the Brain

You can train your brain to rewire itself for positivity through affirmations and practicing gratitude. Research suggests that practicing gratitude can lead to structural changes in the region associated with memory and learning. The strength and growth of these neural connections are linked to an improved ability to adapt to new information and experiences. As gratitude becomes a habit, it shapes the emotional landscape in this network, contributing to an increased capacity for positive emotional experiences and emotional resilience.

Gratitude, much like any skill, can be cultivated and refined through consistent practice. Training your brain is about sculpting neural pathways that predispose you to a more positive and grateful mindset. These intricate networks of interconnected neurons in your brain; known as neural pathways, play a crucial role in the formation of your habits and your behaviors. Repeated gratitude experiences, over time, strengthen and reinforce your neural pathways, making gratitude your natural response.

Use this space to write about the people, the places, and the things in your life that you are grateful for…

_____

_____

_____

_____

_____

_____

_____

Write affirmations to reinforce your gratitude for these people, places, and things

_____

_____

_____

_____

_____

_____

_____

8
Cultivating My Gratitude Practice

Gratitude is a powerful tool for personal growth and resilience. By consciously acknowledging and appreciating the good things around us, we can shift our mindset towards positivity and enhance our overall well-being. This chapter provides exercises to help you develop a deeper awareness of gratitude in your daily life.

Foundation for Cultivating Gratitude

In pursuit of cultivating gratitude and embracing a more fulfilling life, it's essential to establish a strong foundation of self-care and healthy living habits.

Regular Sleep: Ensures optimal emotional regulation and cognitive function.

Nutrition: A balanced diet supports brain health and emotional stability.

Exercise: Enhances mood and reduces anxiety through endorphin release.

Practical Gratitude Exercises

Gratitude Journaling: Write down things you're grateful for daily.

Gratitude Walk: Take mindful walks and focus on your five senses.

Gratitude Jar: Write notes of appreciation and place them in a jar.

Expressing Gratitude: Reach out to someone and express your gratitude.

Three Blessings Exercise

Reflect on positive experiences, meaningful connections, or moments of joy.

What are three things I am grateful for today? and Why?

1. _____
2. _____
3. _____

Why? _____

How did expressing gratitude impact your mood or relationships today?

_____

Elaine Lombardi

Three Blessings Worksheet
copy and print

What are three things you're grateful for today? and **Why?**

1._____

2._____

3._____

Why?_____

_____

How did expressing gratitude impact your mood or relationships today?

_____

What are three things you're grateful for today? and **Why?**

1._____

2._____

3._____

Why?_____

_____

How did expressing gratitude impact your mood or relationships today?

_____

What are three things you're grateful for today? and **Why?**

1._____

2._____

3._____

Why?_____

How did expressing gratitude impact your mood or relationships today?

_____

9
Being the Architect of My Life

Understanding and Trusting Your Intuition

Intuition is a powerful, innate sense that provides clarity and guides you in making choices aligned with your highest potential. It transcends rational thought and connects you to deeper wisdom.

- Intuition goes beyond the five senses, offering insights and inner wisdom.
- It's shaped by experiences, values, and beliefs, serving as a compass in life.
- Learning to trust your intuition involves self-awareness and discernment.
- Practicing self-reflection, meditation, and journaling can enhance intuitive abilities.

Intention is the conscious purpose behind actions. Integrating intuition into your intention-setting process leads to more authentic and fulfilling outcomes. Intuitive Intention is what guides you along your aligned path.

Setting Intuitive Intentions

1. **Choose and write down something your heart desires…**

Example: *"I want to lose 20 pounds so I can feel better and have more energy."*

_____

_____

2. **After writing down what you want, visualize it as already achieved**

Example: Close your eyes and picture yourself feeling and saying the following thought, *"I feel so happy, and I look so amazing. I have so much energy today and love being on my 30-minute walk this morning!"*

3. **Take positive, inspired action toward that goal**

Now go take that walk!

Cultivating a mindset of abundance, gratitude, and belief in your ability to manifest your innermost desires is the first step in achieving what you want. Always focus on positivity, because negativity and self-doubt will block your progress every time. *Just do it!*

The simple act of gazing into a mirror, truly seeing yourself without judgment or criticism, can open the door to profound self-awareness and intuitive wisdom. Through this practice, you can learn to let go of harsh self-judgment and embrace the unique light that shines within you. This heightened self-awareness not only strengthens your intuitive guidance but also enhances your capacity for self-acceptance and self-trust; the foundation for creating lasting transformation from the inside out.

Mirror work can help you cultivate the ability to see yourself through the eyes of your soul, recognizing the light that shines within you. It's a powerful technique used to tap into your inner wisdom and live with intention. It involves looking at yourself in the mirror while affirming positive statements or engaging in self-reflection. By focusing on your reflection, you can connect with your subconscious mind and harness the power of your intuition to set intentions and manifest your desires.

Mirror Work Exercise

1. Find a quiet space with soft lighting.
2. Set a clear intention with an affirmation you will say for your session.
3. Stand or sit comfortably in front of a mirror and make direct eye contact with your reflection.
4. Affirm your intention by saying your affirmation with confidence and conviction.
5. Pay attention to any intuitive insights or feelings that arise.
6. Reflect on your experience and journal any insights.
7. Practice regularly to strengthen your intuition.

Choose one of these Affirmations for your mirror work session (rinse and repeat daily)

"I trust the messages and insights that come through my intuition."

"My intuition is a guiding light that illuminates my authentic path."

"I am confident in my ability to tune into my intuition and make empowered choices."

Self Reflection Questions

What are my core values and passions?

_____

_____

_____

What are my goals and desires?

_____

_____

_____

Visualize

- See your intentions as already manifesting.
- Release doubts and believe in your ability to achieve them.

Take Action

Pursue education, make lifestyle changes, or seek new experiences aligned with your intentions.

Stay Positive:

Maintain an abundance mindset and practice gratitude. By integrating these practices into your life, you can tap into your inner wisdom, set powerful intentions, and manifest a life that aligns with your true self. Trust your intuition, follow your heart, and embrace the endless possibilities that await you.

Crafting a Vision Board

Another powerful tool for manifesting your dreams and goals is to create a vision board. A vision board is a visual representation of your desires. It's a fun and creative process that can help clarify your aspirations and keep you focused on achieving them. It consists of a compilation of images, words, and objects that represent the things you want to achieve or experience in life. By creating a vision board and placing it in a visible place, you can constantly be reminded of your goals and stay motivated to work towards them.

10
My Ego vs My Soul

Understanding the difference between ego-driven desires and soul-aligned intentions is key to living a fulfilling and purpose-driven life. This involves self-awareness and introspection to identify motivations that stem from superficial wants versus those that resonate with your true essence.

Ego-Driven Desires:

- Seek external validation and immediate gratification.
- Fueled by fear, comparison, and societal expectations.
- Often leads to temporary satisfaction and inner conflict.

Soul-Aligned Intentions:

- Stem from inner wisdom and core values.
- Seek genuine growth, fulfillment, and alignment with true self.
- Provide lasting fulfillment and inner peace.

Self Reflection Questions

What are my core values, and how do they guide my decisions?

_____

_____

When have I acted from a place of ego rather than soul?

_____

_____

How can I better align my actions with my core values?

_____

_____

11
Self-Sabotaging Behaviors

Self-sabotaging behaviors hinder progress, goals, and overall happiness. They often stem from underlying issues or beliefs about yourself or the world around you. Some common self-sabotaging behaviors include negative self-talk, where you constantly criticize yourself and question your abilities. Negative addictive behaviors serve as self-punishment.

Self-Reflection Questions

Self-sabotaging behaviors can manifest in various aspects of life, including relationships, career, health, and personal development. Often, the underlying psychological factors at play are fear of failure, low self-esteem, perfectionism, or a deep-seated belief that you are unworthy of success and happiness.

What self-sabotaging behaviors have I or do I tend to engage in?

_____

What underlying triggers, fears, or beliefs might be driving these behaviors?

_____

Practical Steps to Overcome Self-Sabotage

1. **Self-Awareness**: Recognize triggers and patterns in your behavior.
2. **Emotional Regulation**: Practice mindfulness and constructive expression of emotions.
3. **Positive Affirmations**: Reinforce positive beliefs about yourself.
4. **Supportive Relationships**: Surround yourself with positive influences.
5. **Mindfulness and Reflection**: Regularly assess and adjust your behaviors and beliefs.

What strategies will you use to overcome your self-sabotaging behavior?

_____

_____

_____

By understanding and addressing self-sabotaging behaviors, you can unlock your full potential and pursue a more fulfilling and authentic life.

12
My Relationship with Family and Friends

Family and friends significantly shape who you are, influencing your personality and life experiences. They play both positive and negative roles in your development.

Self Reflection Questions

Recognizing the impact of family and friends allows you to cultivate supportive relationships and set boundaries when needed, promoting personal growth and well-being.

How does my family influence my values and beliefs?

_____
_____
_____
_____
_____

What role do my friends play in my life?

_____
_____
_____
_____
_____

How do I contribute to my family dynamics?

_____
_____
_____
_____
_____

Journaling Exercise

Write about a positive experience with your family.

_____
_____
_____
_____
_____
_____
_____

What did I learn from it?

_____
_____
_____

Reflect on a time when a friend supported you through a difficult situation.

_____
_____
_____
_____
_____
_____
_____

How did it impact me?

_____
_____
_____
_____

Elaine Lombardi

Describe a challenge you faced in your family and how you overcame it.

_____
_____
_____
_____
_____
_____
_____
_____
_____
_____
_____
_____
_____

What did I learn about myself?

_____
_____
_____
_____
_____
_____
_____
_____
_____

13
My Personality Development

Your personality is shaped by genetic, biological, and environmental factors. Genetics play a crucial role, as you inherit traits that influence temperament and behavior. Brain chemistry and neurobiology also impact personality through neurotransmitters like serotonin and dopamine, which affect mood and traits. Hormones such as estrogen, testosterone, cortisol, and oxytocin regulate mood and behavior, contributing to personality development.

Environmental influences include early experiences, especially childhood attachments, which foster trust and confidence. Family dynamics shape behavior and personality, while social interactions and cultural context provide a framework for learning social norms and values. Life events like moving, loss, or achieving milestones also shape personality, as responses to these events contribute to development.

Psychological factors, including thoughts and beliefs, significantly impact personality. Optimistic thoughts enhance mood and self-worth, while pessimistic thoughts lead to anxiety and low self-esteem. Self-awareness and cognitive reframing help cultivate a positive mindset. Attitudes, reflecting beliefs, guide behavior and shape personality.

Personality disorders illustrate how deviations from typical personality patterns can cause distress and impairment. Early intervention and personalized treatment improve quality of life.

Self Reflection Exercise

Reflect on your personality development

Early Experiences: Write about a significant early experience that shaped your personality. How did it influence your behavior and self-view?

_____
_____
_____
_____
_____
_____
_____

Genetic Influences: Consider traits inherited from your parents. How do these traits manifest in your daily life and interactions?

_____
_____
_____
_____

Social Interactions: Reflect on a key social interaction that impacted your personality. What did you learn, and how has it shaped your view of yourself and others?

_____
_____
_____
_____

Life Events: Describe a major life event that influenced your personality. How did you respond, and what changes did it bring about?

_____
_____
_____
_____

Thoughts and Beliefs: Identify a recurring thought or belief about yourself. How does it influence your actions and interactions? How might you reframe this thought to promote a more positive self-view?

_____
_____
_____
_____

14
Self-Worth, Self-Confidence, and Self-Esteem

Self-worth, self-confidence, and self-esteem define how you perceive and value yourself. They are interconnected but distinct.

Self-Worth: Self-worth is a deep sense of self-respect and acceptance. It means valuing yourself without relying on external achievements or approval. You accept your strengths and weaknesses, recognizing your inherent value. This acceptance helps set healthy boundaries and fosters resilience. Developing self-worth involves self-awareness, self-compassion, and supportive relationships.

Self-Confidence: Self-confidence is the belief in your abilities and judgment. It stems from a positive self-perception and realistic appraisal of your strengths. Self-confidence encourages independence, resilience, and risk-taking. It is developed through achievements and positive reinforcement. Building self-confidence involves stepping out of your comfort zone, setting achievable goals, and celebrating victories.

Self-Esteem: Self-esteem is your evaluation of your worth and value. It involves self-acceptance, self-respect, and self-love. Healthy self-esteem leads to a positive self-image and belief in your abilities. It is influenced by early experiences, relationships, and personal achievements. Cultivating self-esteem requires self-awareness, self-compassion, and intentional self-care.

Self Reflection Exercise

Reflect on your self-worth, self-confidence, and self-esteem.

Early Experiences: Write about a significant early experience that shaped your self-worth. How did it influence your sense of value and acceptance?

_____

_____

_____

_____

_____

_____

_____

Elaine Lombardi

Achievements: Describe an achievement that boosted your self-confidence. What did you learn about your abilities and strengths?

_____
_____
_____
_____

Self-Image: Reflect on your current self-esteem. How do you view yourself, and what factors contribute to this perception?

_____
_____
_____
_____
_____

Boundaries: Identify an area in your life where you need to set boundaries. How will setting these boundaries protect your well-being and enhance your self-worth?

_____
_____
_____
_____
_____

Positive Affirmations: Write down three positive affirmations about yourself. Reflect on how repeating these affirmations can improve your self-esteem and self-confidence.

1. _____
2. _____
3. _____

15
Strengthening My Communication

Building genuine connections with family and friends requires trust, openness, and understanding. Being authentic in your interactions fosters deeper relationships. Embracing vulnerability by sharing your joys and struggles creates trust and empathy. This type of open communication is crucial for meaningful connections.

Open Communication: Be transparent and honest in your interactions. Avoid hiding your true thoughts or feelings. Respect boundaries and celebrate individuality to foster authenticity.

Effective Communication: Effective communication is the cornerstone of healthy relationships. It involves clear expression and active listening. Use "I" statements, and pay attention to nonverbal cues. Improving communication enhances understanding and strengthens emotional connections.

Yes No

[ ] [ ] Do you feel comfortable expressing your true thoughts and feelings with family and friends?

[ ] [ ] Are there topics you avoid discussing with loved ones?

[ ] [ ] Do you actively listen to others without interrupting?

[ ] [ ] Are you able to set and communicate boundaries effectively?

[ ] [ ] Do you use "I" statements to express your feelings and needs?

[ ] [ ] Do you feel heard and understood by your loved ones?

[ ] [ ] Are you able to empathize with others' perspectives during conversations?

[ ] [ ] Do you find it challenging to engage in meaningful conversations?

Evaluate Your Communication Skills

Reflect on your communication strengths and weaknesses. Identify specific areas to improve and consider how these changes might positively affect your relationships.

_____
_____
_____
_____

16
Strategies for a Healthy, Long-Lasting Relationship

Regardless of your relationship status or orientation—single, married, divorced, or LGBTQ, the core principles of a loving and healthy relationship remain consistent. Here are key strategies to foster and maintain a fulfilling partnership:

Open and Honest Communication

At the heart of any strong relationship lies open and honest communication. This open dialogue fosters deep connection and intimacy.

Love and Kindness

Love should permeate every aspect of your relationship. It manifests through thoughtful gestures, creating a harmonious balance of give and take and uplifting one another.

Trust

Trust is the bedrock of a healthy relationship. Partners need to rely on each other, knowing their vulnerabilities will be respected and their secrets kept sacred.

Mutual Respect

Mutual respect involves recognizing and appreciating each other's unique strengths and differences. Support each other's dreams, ambitions, and personal growth, understanding that individual successes contribute to the relationship's collective success.

Intimacy

Intimacy, both physical and emotional, is vital. Emotional intimacy runs deeper as you share your innermost thoughts, fears, and hopes, creating a safe haven where both partners feel truly known and accepted.

Friendship and Companionship

Partners in a healthy relationship are best friends, confidants, and lifelong companions facing life's challenges together. Your love should be a source of strength, resilience, and inspiration.

Journaling Exercise

Write about a recent conversation with your partner where you felt truly understood or misunderstood.

_____
_____
_____
_____
_____
_____
_____
_____

What made the difference?

_____
_____
_____

How can you apply this understanding to improve future conversations?

_____
_____
_____
_____

Consider the level of trust in your relationship. Are there areas where trust could be improved?

_____
_____
_____
_____
_____

Journal about specific actions you can take to build or rebuild trust with your partner.

_____
_____
_____
_____
_____
_____
_____

Write about ways to cultivate and celebrate intimacy regularly.

_____
_____
_____
_____
_____
_____
_____

Describe a recent fun activity or shared experience with your partner.

_____
_____
_____
_____
_____
_____
_____

How did it enhance your friendship and connection?

_____
_____
_____
_____
_____
_____
_____

Plan and journal about future activities that could bring you closer.

_____
_____
_____
_____
_____
_____
_____
_____

Things to Talk About with Your Partner

- What aspects of our relationship are working well and bring us joy and satisfaction?
- What areas of our relationship could use improvement or more attention?
- Are there specific changes or goals we would like to achieve together to strengthen our bond?
- How can we enhance our communication to ensure we both feel heard and understood?
- What steps can we take to deepen our emotional and physical intimacy?
- How can we better support each other's individual dreams, goals, and personal growth?

17
My Knowledge and Wisdom

In various stages of life, many people find themselves at a crossroads, especially when major life changes occur, such as children gaining independence or transitioning into retirement. This period can bring about feelings of restlessness and a yearning for deeper purpose and personal growth. The following explores how to embrace this transformative phase and find new passions that bring fulfillment and joy.

Embracing New Passions

Returning to school or pursuing new certifications can be a powerful way to reignite your sense of purpose. Delving into new ventures and fields of interest, often leads to personal growth and can significantly impact your mindset and approach to life.

Navigating Challenges with Resilience

Life is unpredictable, and challenges are inevitable. Whether it's dealing with the declining health of a loved one, facing a personal health crisis, or navigating other unexpected life events, these experiences test our resilience and ability to adapt. By utilizing newly acquired skills, knowledge, and mindfulness practices, you can manage these challenges with greater ease and compassion.

Finding New Avenues for Fulfillment

Exploring new hobbies, traveling, or engaging in community activities can bring a renewed sense of purpose.

Journaling Exercise

What activities or subjects have recently sparked your interest?

_____
_____
_____
_____
_____
_____
_____

How do you plan to explore these new interests further?

_____
_____
_____

In what ways can you share your knowledge and insights with those around you?

_____
_____
_____
_____
_____
_____
_____
_____
_____

What new goals or aspirations do you have for the next phase of your life?

_____
_____
_____

What steps will you take to achieve these goals, and how will they contribute to your sense of purpose?

_____
_____
_____
_____
_____
_____

18
Journey to Unlock My Treasured Wisdom

Your MISSION, should you choose to accept it is to go on a quest to unlock your treasure chest of knowledge and wisdom to discover the life-changing GIFTS within.

19
My Best Day Ever!

20
Self-Love & Care

Self-love and self-care are foundational for overall well-being. These practices encompass physical, emotional, mental, and spiritual aspects, creating a balanced and fulfilling life.

What physical activities make you feel rejuvenated and energized?

_____
_____
_____

How can you incorporate more of these activities into your routine?

_____
_____
_____

What practices can you adopt to better honor and express your feelings?

_____
_____
_____

What activities help clear your mind and reduce stress?

_____
_____
_____

What activities connect you to your deeper values and purpose?

_____
_____
_____

21
Rejuvenating Sleep Ritual

Quality sleep is essential for health and well-being. Establishing a sleep ritual can enhance the quality of your sleep.

Five Simple Steps to Better Sleep

1. Avoid stimulants like caffeine, alcohol, and electronics 2 hours before bed.
2. Create a sleep sanctuary environment that's cool, dark, quiet, and comfortable.
3. Engage in relaxing light body stretches, breathwork, or a warm bath
4. Keep a worry journal by your bed to jot down any thoughts that keep you awake
5. Stick to a consistent sleep/wake schedule, even on weekends

What is your current bedtime routine?

_____
_____
_____
_____

How well do you sleep on a regular basis?

_____
_____
_____
_____

What changes can you make to your environment to improve sleep?

_____
_____
_____
_____

22
Mindful Healthy Eating Habits

A balanced diet rich in whole foods provides your body with the vitamins, minerals, antioxidants, fiber, and other vital nutrients it needs to function at its best. Prioritize eating plenty of fruits, vegetables, whole grains, lean proteins, healthy fats, and drinking sufficient water. These minimally processed foods deliver maximum nutritional value.

Healthy Eating Guidelines

Focus on a Balanced Diet

- Include a variety of food groups (proteins, carbohydrates, fats, fruits, and vegetables) in each meal.
- Aim for colorful plates with diverse nutrients.

Portion Control

- Be mindful of portion sizes to avoid overeating.
- Use smaller plates to help control portions naturally.

Regular Meal Times

- Establish consistent meal times to regulate your body's hunger signals.
- Avoid skipping meals to maintain energy levels throughout the day.

Hydration

- Drink plenty of water throughout the day.
- Limit sugary drinks and excessive caffeine.

Whole Foods

- Focus on whole, unprocessed foods for the majority of your meals.
- Minimize intake of processed and packaged foods high in added sugars and unhealthy fats.

Healthy Snacks

- Choose nutrient-dense snacks like fruits, nuts, yogurt, or vegetables.
- Plan ahead to have healthy snacks available when needed.

Cooking at Home

- Prepare meals at home to have better control over ingredients and cooking methods.
- Experiment with new recipes to keep meals interesting and enjoyable.

Limiting Sugar and Salt

- Reduce the amount of added sugars and salt in your diet.
- Read food labels to be aware of hidden sugars and sodium.

Self Reflection Questions

Are you eating a well-balanced, colorful, whole foods diet? If not what will you do to improve your eating habits?

_____
_____
_____

Beyond just eating nutritious whole foods, promote healthy digestion by focusing on a relaxed eating environment, chewing thoroughly, avoiding excessive liquid intake with meals, and not rushing through your food. Eat slowly and mindfully to naturally tune into your body's satiety cues. Focus on what, how, and when you eat.

Mindful Eating

- Eat slowly and savor each bite, paying attention to flavors and textures.
- Avoid distractions like TV or smartphones while eating.

Listening to Your Body

- Pay attention to your body's hunger and fullness cues.
- Eat when you're hungry and stop when you're satisfied.

How well do you listen to your body's hunger and fullness cues?

_____
_____
_____
_____

23
Exercise Plan Made Easy

Regular physical activity is crucial for maintaining overall health and well-being. Exercise helps improve cardiovascular health, strengthen muscles, enhance flexibility, and boost mental health. Developing a consistent exercise routine can be both enjoyable and sustainable when tailored to your preferences and lifestyle.

Finding enjoyable ways to move makes exercise more sustainable. It's beneficial to break exercise into two categories: functional and planned workouts. Functional movement exercises include taking the stairs instead of the elevator, and parking at the far end of the parking lot when going shopping. Planned exercise includes going to the gym, strength training, and activities like hiking. Be mindful of balancing your workouts and activities for both enjoyment and progression.

A Sample Exercise Plan

- **Monday**
  - **Cardio:** 30-minute brisk walk or jog.
  - **Strength:** 15 minutes of bodyweight exercises (e.g., squats, push-ups, planks).

- **Tuesday**
  - **Flexibility:** 30-minute yoga session.
  - **Recreational:** 20 minutes of dancing or a fun sport.

- **Wednesday**
  - **Cardio:** 20 minutes of cycling or swimming.
  - **Strength:** 15 minutes of resistance band exercises.

- **Thursday**
  - **Flexibility:** 20 minutes of stretching exercises.
  - **Recreational:** 30 minutes of gardening or hiking.

- **Friday**
  - **Cardio:** 25-minute run or aerobic exercise.
  - **Strength:** 20 minutes of weight lifting or bodyweight exercises.

- **Saturday**
  - **Flexibility:** 30-minute Pilates session.
  - **Recreational:** 40 minutes of playing a favorite sport or outdoor activity.

- **Sunday**
  - **Rest Day:** Allow your body to rest and recover. Engage in light activities.

Self Reflection Questions

What types of exercises do you enjoy?

_____

_____

24
Personal Care

Creating a nurturing self-care plan is an act of embracing deep self-love and compassion. It involves restructuring your daily, weekly, and monthly routine and shaping a life filled with nourishing habits that treat your mind, body, and spirit as precious priorities.

Among those habits should be the rhythm of practicing deep breathing for tranquility and centeredness followed by gentle cleansing and skin brushing to increase circulation and lymph flow, and help remove toxins that can accumulate over time. Personal care routines contribute to overall well-being and confidence.

Self Reflection Questions

What does your current personal care routine look like?

_____
_____
_____
_____

What aspects of personal care are most important to you?

_____
_____
_____
_____

How well are these needs being met?

_____
_____
_____
_____

25
Designing A Nurturing Self-Care Plan

Making self-love and self-care a priority allows you to show up as your best self in all areas of life. Designing an intentional self nurturing plan can help ensure you are carving out that vital time for replenishing your mind, body, and spirit.

The checklist provided below is a general guide containing items you may consider including in your daily, weekly, and monthly care plan. It's important to customize these practices to align with your individual preferences and needs. When tailoring your plan, prioritize simplicity and efficiency. Aim to create a routine that feels natural and easy to follow, minimizing complexity and maximizing effectiveness.

Mind-Body-Spirt Care Checklist Physical Self-Care

- ☐ Regular exercise routine that aligns with your fitness goals and preferences.
- ☐ Balanced and nutritious diet to nourish your body.
- ☐ Sufficient and quality sleep for optimal rest and recovery.
- ☐ Hydration – ensure you're drinking an adequate amount of water daily.

Emotional and Mental Well-Being

- ☐ Daily mindfulness or meditation practice for stress reduction.
- ☐ Journaling to express and reflect on your thoughts and emotions.
- ☐ Time for hobbies and activities that bring you joy and relaxation.
- ☐ Establish healthy boundaries to protect your emotional well-being.

Social Connections

- ☐ Regular quality time with friends and loved ones.
- ☐ Engage in activities that foster social connections.
- ☐ Communicate openly and honestly in your relationships.
- ☐ Seek support when needed and nurture positive connections.

Personal Development

- ☐ Set and work towards personal and professional goals.
- ☐ Continuous learning and skill development.
- ☐ Reading or consuming content that inspires and motivates you.
- ☐ Reflection on your values and life purpose.

Rest and Relaxation

☐ Scheduled downtime for rest and relaxation.

☐ Regular breaks during work or daily tasks.

☐ Incorporate activities that promote relaxation, such as baths or walks in nature.

☐ Practice deep breathing or other relaxation techniques

Self-Compassion and Positive Affirmations

☐ Positive self-talk and affirmations.

☐ Cultivate self-compassion in moments of challenge.

☐ Forgive yourself for mistakes and imperfections.

☐ Celebrate achievements, no matter how small.

Skincare and Grooming

☐ Establish a skincare routine that suits your skin type.

☐ Grooming activities that make you feel good about your appearance.

☐ Self-care practices like massages or spa treatments.

Digital Detox

☐ Set boundaries on screen time.

☐ Schedule regular breaks from social media.

☐ Disconnect from devices before bedtime.

Regular Self-Reflection

☐ Periodically review and adjust your self-love and care routine.

☐ Assess what's working well and what might need improvement.

☐ Stay attuned to changes in your needs and priorities.

Is there anything else you'd like to add?

_____

_____

_____

_____

_____

26
My Path to Purpose, Passion, Joy, and Fulfillment

Living a truly fulfilling life involves discovering your purpose, pursuing your passions, and cultivating sustained joy. When you align your purpose with your passions, you can create a life filled with meaning, joy, and fulfillment.

Discovering Your Life's Purpose

Your life purpose is the compass that guides you. It represents your core values and the positive impact you want to make on the world around you

What activities make you feel most alive and inspired? Reflect on moments when you felt deeply fulfilled. What were you doing?

_____
_____
_____
_____
_____
_____

Pursuing Your Passions

Passion encompasses the interests, hobbies, career paths, and creative pursuits that you find deeply engaging and fulfilling.

What hobbies or interests bring you the most joy? How can you make more time for activities you are passionate about?

_____
_____
_____
_____
_____

Cultivating Sustained Joy

While fleeting pleasures provide momentary happiness, the path to sustained, soul-level joy is walking in alignment with your purpose and passions.

What practices help you feel grateful and joyful? How can you serve others in a way that aligns with your talents?

_____

_____

_____

_____

Crafting Your Fulfilling Life

Discovering and honoring your life's purpose takes courage, self reflection, and commitment.

What steps can you take to prioritize what matters most to you? How can you let go of inauthentic demands and live more intentionally?

_____

_____

_____

_____

Action Steps

Identify one passion you want to pursue more actively and make a plan to integrate it into your life.

_____

Set a goal related to your purpose that you can work towards in the next month.

_____

Create a gratitude journal to regularly reflect on the aspects of your life that bring you joy.

_____

Conclusion

The keys to unlocking your highest self have been placed firmly in your grasp. Through your courageous inner exploration, you've awakened the dormant gifts that lay within your appreciative spirit, the trust in your instincts, your capacity for deep connection, the wellspring of your life's lessons, and your unshakable self-acceptance. Carry your gifts forth as embodied strengths now.

Pause for a moment and reflect on how far you've come. The path has not been easy; confronting wounds, limiting beliefs, and embracing profound truths about yourself requires tremendous courage. But you persisted, motivated by a deep yearning to unlock your full potential and live a life of purpose, passion, and fulfillment. You now carry within you the keys that unlock the treasure chests of G.I.F.T.S. to a life of boundless possibilities.

1. The key to the gift of gratitude has awakened you to the beauty that surrounds you each day.
2. Intuitive intentions have realigned you with your authentic self.
3. Nurturing your cherished relationships with family and friends has provided a bedrock of love and support.
4. Embracing your treasured, hard-won wisdom has given you the resilience to face life's challenges with grace.
5. And, above all, living in your truth through radical self-love and care has been the greatest act of revolution and the dismantling of the chains that once bound you.

As you step forward, let this not be an ending, but a new beginning. A renaissance of your soul. You are the master of your destiny, the author of your life's greatest story. Nurture the dreams that once flickered like distant stars as they now blaze brilliantly within your grasp. Pursue your passions with unbridled enthusiasm, for they will be the compass guiding you to profound happiness, joy, and fulfillment.

You are a phenomenal human being, blessed with infinite gifts yearning to be expressed and shared with a world that desperately needs your light. Wherever the currents of life may take you, carry this empowering truth:

> *"You have everything you need to soar into your limitless potential and create a life that is a breathtaking masterpiece."*

The possibilities are bound only by the borders of your imagination. So let your spirit soar into its greatness. Live boldly. Love fiercely. Experience life's majesty. You are the artist and the canvas awaits your brushstrokes of brilliant radiant color. Take this day, and all the ones that follow, and paint the masterpiece of your dreams. I believe in you!

About The Author

Elaine Lombardi is a seasoned travel enthusiast with over seven decades of rich experiences and stories. Through her journey, she's learned the invaluable art of transforming life lessons into wisdom, a gift she believes everyone holds.

With a heart full of passion, Elaine ventured into the realm of online education, striving to empower women to rediscover their strengths, share their unique stories, and leave a legacy that resonates.

Elaine Lombardi is a certified CHHC holistic health coach. With a focus on nutrition, her training at the Institute for Integrative Nutrition included all aspects of well-being as an AADP Board Certified Practitioner by the American Association of Drugless Practitioners.

Aside from her coaching practice, she worked with young adults on the autism spectrum as an Occupational Counselor for the State of California teaching independent living skills, and helping to transition them from living at home to living on their own. Other certifications she holds include Reiki, EFT, Reflexology, American Red Cross Water Safety Instructor, AFAA Aerobics and Fitness Association of America, and Family and Consumer Studies ECE Early Childhood Education Private Agency Certified Preschool Teacher and Director.

Married 52 years, she resides in southern California with her husband Michael and rescue dog Frankie. They are the proud parents of four grown children, grandparents of ten grandchildren, and two great-grandbabies. Elaine enjoys world travel, camping painting, and writing.

Her other published books include:

Hurricane Lucy A Caregiver's Guide

Little Lessons, Big Life Journal

Big Teddy Bear: The Colorful New Arrivals

www.ingramcontent.com/pod-product-compliance
Lightning Source LLC
Chambersburg PA
CBHW060530010526
44110CB00052B/2557